A⌊
P⌊

Nicholas Tomihama

Levi Dream Publishing

PUBLISHED BY LEVI DREAM, 2011

LEVI DREAM PUBLISHING, P.O. BOX 75203, HONOLULU, HI 96836-0203

PRINTED IN THE U.S.A., CHARLESTON, SC

FIRST PRINTING IN 2011

ISBN: 978-0-9832481-3-2

LIBRARY OF CONGRESS CATALOGING-IN-PUBLICATION DATA IS
AVAILABLE ON FILE.

For my wife Angela, my son Levi, and all those I am honored to call friend by birth or bond.

"A man of many companions may come to ruin, but there is a friend who sticks closer than a brother."
-Proverbs 18:24

Table of Contents

Chapter 0
6 - the Intro - 6

Chapter 1
9 - the Basics - 9

Chapter 2
35 - the Survival Bracelet - 35

Chapter 3
55 - the Paracord Bracelet - 55

Chapter 4
68 - the Watch Band - 68

Table of Contents

Chapter 5
89 - <u>Keychains</u> - 89

Chapter 6
102 - <u>Lanyards and Straps</u> - 104

Chapter 7
114 - <u>Cord Wrapping</u> - 114

132 - <u>Thank You</u> - 132

133 - <u>About the Author</u> - 133

Chapter VII
134 - <u>Bonus Track</u> - 134

CHAPTER 0
THE INTRO

There are many opportunities open to those who embark on the life-altering (and usually expensive) adventure known commonly as College. Depending on your strengths, abilities, knowledge, and skill/ineptitude with the opposite sex, you could embark on many a journey.

Some immerse themselves in the academia and come out on top of the class, most likely to get a good paying job and hefty student loans. Some opt for a lighter load, preferring the party scene, the sex scene, and/or the drug scene. Some strive for athletic perfection and the shot at a multi-billion dollar professional sport contract.

What did I do? I made stuff. Lots of stuff. Mainly stuff that could be made safely (or at least reasonably so... most of the time, anyway) in the confines of your standard dorm room. While my room mate pondered the depths of shroom-induced introspection or floated among cannabis clouds, I was hard at work crafting things with my hands, like the hook over to your left.

I also spent a lot of time at the local army surplus store,

where I not only found a plethora of tools and gadgets to make bone carving and forest exploration (I mean actually exploring a forest. There is no innuendo here) much easier. I also found Paracord.

Paracord, or parachute cord, was once used in parachutes as the name implies. Since its early days, it has grown in popularity for its usefulness, a usefulness perhaps near or even exceeding that of duct tape. It can be found virtually everywhere, from sporting goods stores to surplus stores, and even perhaps in your grandfather's basement.

While there are many types of cord, this book uses 550 Type III cord, MIL-C-5040 Type III cord (this fits military specifications for fit, finish, and a consistent weight-bearing), and 650 Paraline. 550 Type III and Mil-Spec Type III are nearly identical, with a breaking strength of 550 pounds. The main difference is that Mil-Spec is usually more consistent as it is manufactured to government specifications. 650 cord is much weaker, only having a breaking strength around 300 pounds or so.

The big difference in weight-bearing between 550 and 650 is due to the internal strands used in the cord. All three cords use basically the same outer shell, which has about a 200 pound breaking strength. In 550 cord, which is on the left, the

core is made up of seven tightly woven, two-ply strands. In 650 cord, which is on the right, the core is composed of roughly four or so strands of fluffy nylon. In some cases, and depending on manufacturer, it may be just nylon-fiber filling.

550 cord is superior for practical and survival use. It is very tough and can be used for tie-downs, for lifting and dragging heavy objects, supporting human weight if need be, and many other applications. The internal strands are also useful for sewing, lashing, and any application a smaller thread is called for.

As far as braiding and wrapping goes, 650 Paraline is a better choice because the fluffy fibers make the cord fuller and less likely to cause bunching or twisting when braided. All of the instructions in the book are photographs of 650 cord, though the same instructions apply to 550 cord.

Once you've got some cord, and really, any cord can be used for this, not only paracord, you are ready to start. Almost all of the projects in this book are based off of the simple cobra knot. In the first chapter, we'll go over how to do the cobra knot and a few other basic things.

All of these braiding projects are fairly easy to do, and the materials are fairly easy to come by. Old backpacks and laptop/camera cases are great places to scrounge side-release buckles and other metal findings. Some craft and general supply stores also sell items like buckles, key rings, clasps, and other assorted items.

This book contains only a few possible things you can do with paracord, it is truly a versatile material. Once you get the hang of it, there is really no limit to what you can come up with. With that said, let's get started.

CHAPTER 1
THE BASICS

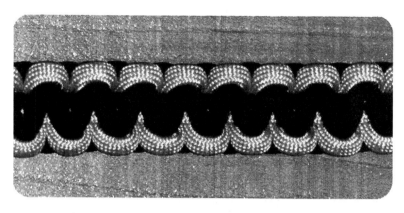

Welcome to chapter one, THE BASICS. Like the title implies, this chapter is about building the foundation for the rest of the book. We will go over how to tie the Cobra Knot, which is the basis of all the different bracelets and things.

This chapter will also cover how to finish the cobra knot, how to tie a decorative lanyard knot, how to splice two colors of cord together, and how to make a simple sliding toggle using the cobra knot.

Cobra Knot

The cobra knot, also called a square knot, is very simple to master. It is essentially an overhand knot repeated in different directions over a core. It may seem a little confusing at first, but with a little practice it will become second nature. I find myself doing this knot all the time if I happen to find a piece of rope, string, or even grass in my hands.

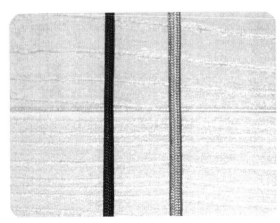

Start with two cords, side by side. We'll call the black one A, the gray one B.

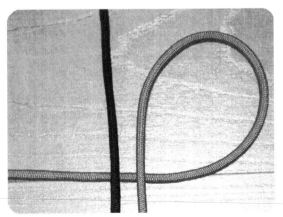

Take side B and create a loop, bringing the end under both cords like in the picture.

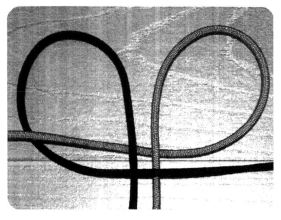

Loop side A, bringing it under the end of side B and then over both of the central cords.

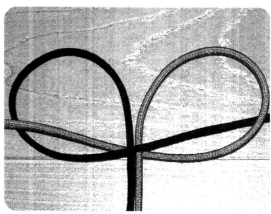

Tuck the end of side A under the side B loop as shown, making both sides appear even.

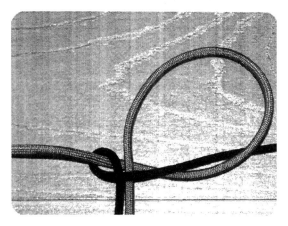

Start tightening by pulling the end of side A.

Finish the beginning knot by pulling side B through and tightening both sides.

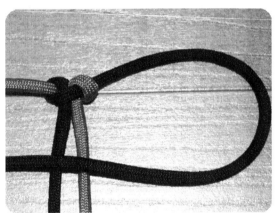

Now, repeat the last few steps, except as a mirror-image. Start by looping side A over the two cords.

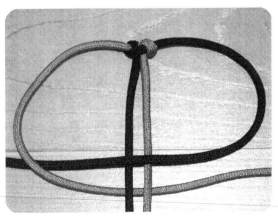

Loop side B over the end of side A and under the central cords.

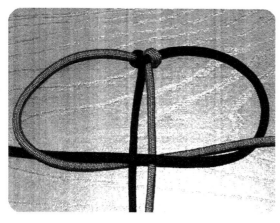

Tuck the end of side B through the side A loop, bringing it over the loop from the inside.

Tighten both sides, forming the second knot.

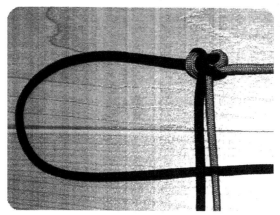

Now do the exact thing you did in the first step. Order doesn't really matter, just make sure that side A goes over the cords and side B goes under.

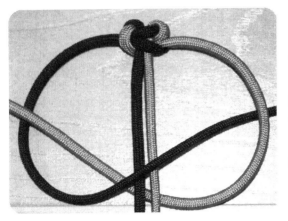

Also make sure the ends of the cords go through the opposite loops. Side A goes into the side B loop and under side B, side B goes into the side A loop and over side A.

Now that the third knot is complete, treat the next one like the second knot, then keep alternating sides until you have completed the length of your knots.

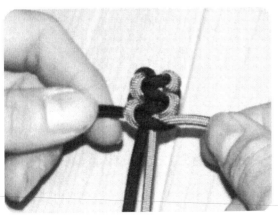

From over my shoulder, watch as I make a few knots. To help you get started, notice that side A is coming out of the back of the side B loop.

If you turned the piece over, you would see gray bars and black loops instead of black bars and gray loops. The end that comes out of the loop (side A) is the one that goes over the central cords.

Take the side without a loop, in this case side B, and tuck it under the central cords.

Pass the ends of each cord through the opposite loop.

Pull both ends tight. Be sure you are pulling your knots tight and consistently, or the finished stack of knots will appear uneven and messy.

Once you've gotten the hang of it, go ahead and get started on something! As a side note, a long line of these knots make good straps for belts, slings, guitar straps, etc., on their own.

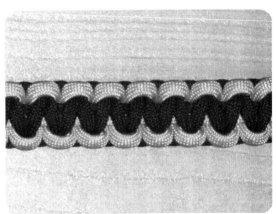

FINISHING THE KNOT

Once you've tied your Cobra knot as far down as you want it, the ends remain loose. One simple way to finish the knot is to tie two overhand knots, locking the cord in place. If you want a more clean and neat appearance, there are three ways to finish the knot. The first is to simply melt the ends of the cord, the second is to tuck the ends under the knots, and the final is to tie a knot in each end.

Melting the ends is exactly how it sounds. Once you've finished knotting, pull the ends tight and cut them off, leaving about $^1/_8$ of an inch sticking out of each end.

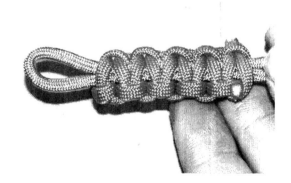

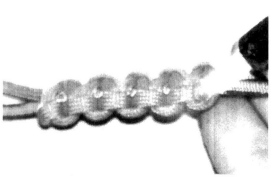

With a lighter, match, or other heat source, heat one end until the end beads up and looks slightly molten. Try to not set it on fire or burn it.

Once molten, the end will spread out, like the head of a nail. This will keep the end from coming apart, and keep the exposed cord from fraying.

Simply melting the end will leave you with a raised bump. If you want to, smooth it out with your finger dipped into a little bit of cold water.

You will hear a hiss and the cord end will flatten like this. This is what a melted end should look like.

There are many ways to tuck the ends of the finished knot under itself. This one is the easiest in that it does not require pliers or any sewing, and is less time consuming than simply pulling each end up by hand.

Start by taking a length of paracord and laying it down on your stack of knot like in the picture. The ends of the cord should be long enough for you to pull on them. About five or six inches is good.

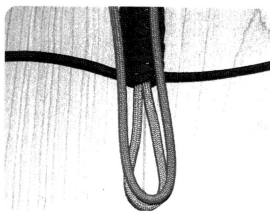

Loosely finish tying knots until you have reached the end.

Like this.

Take the ends of the finished knot and pass them through the loop.

Pull the loop up and tight. Make sure the ends of the finished knot are left slightly loose, to give room for them to be pulled under the knots.

20 FINISHING THE KNOT - TUCKING UNDER

Keep pulling until the ends come free.

With the ends free, tighten the end of the finished knot starting from top to bottom, much like you would tighten shoe laces.

Once the end is tight, simply trim the two cords and hide the ends under the other knots.

Finishing the Knot - Tucking Under 21

This final method is the easiest way to finish cords of any type, as some cords do not melt, and some will simply come apart if tucked under.

Pull both ends tight, then tie an overhand knot into one end.

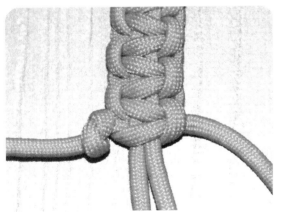

Tighten the knot, pressing it as close as possible into the main body of the cobra stitch.

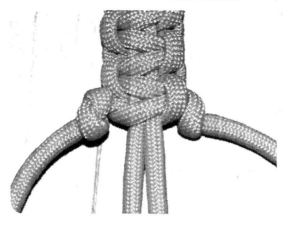

Repeat on the other side and make sure both sides are tight.

You could either leave the ends hanging free, which can add some decorative flair, or cut and melt them like in the picture. Here is the completed end.

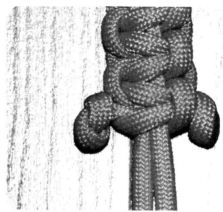

LANYARD KNOT

The lanyard knot is a common knot used to finish the ends of lanyards and other decorative items. I prefer this knot because it is fairly small, easily moved around before final tightening, and adds a clean, finished look as opposed to simply tying an overhand knot. This knot requires a few extra inches of cord to pull off, so plan your projects accordingly.

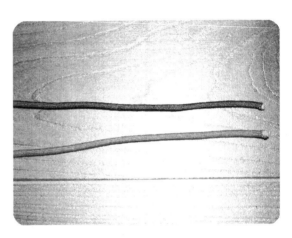

Start by laying the ends of your two cords, side by side. The darker cord is side A, the lighter side B.

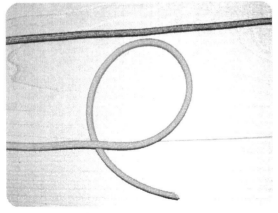

Take cord B and form a loop, placing the end of the loop under the cord.

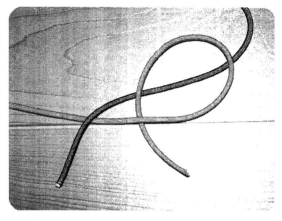

Take cord A and bring it down and around, going under the loop and over the long end of cord B.

Bring the end of A under the end of B.

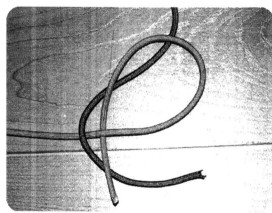

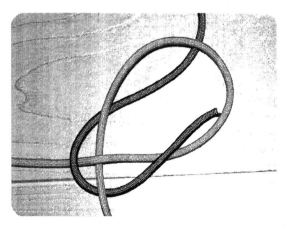

Bring the end of A over the bottom of the loop cord B made.

LANYARD KNOT 25

Pass the end of A under itself, forming a loop.

Bring the end of A over the B loop. This should make both loops look similar, like in the picture. Once you get the hang of the knot, it is much easier to simply pass the two loops together.

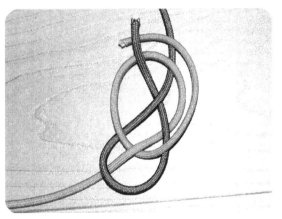

Take the end of B and bring it around over the long side of A and under the short side of A.

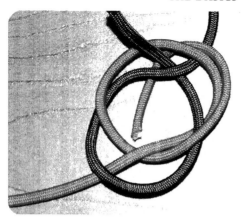

Bring the end of B into the center formed by the two loops, and pull it up.

Pull it to the side so it stays out of the way.

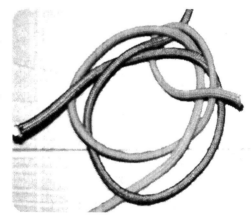

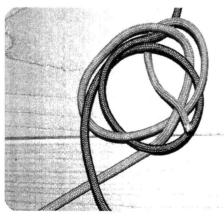

Bring the end of A around and over the long end of B.

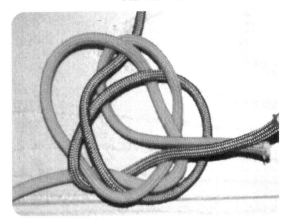

Bring the short end of A under the loop and through the center with the short side of B.

Take both cords and pull slightly, then shift the cords around till the knot is centered where you want it. Then pull the cords tight.

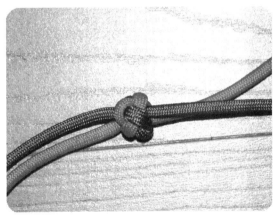

Here is the finished knot. It takes a little bit of adjusting and shifting to tighten it up, but once it is, the finished knot is clean and attractive.

Two Cord Splice

If you have multiple colors of paracord, a nice effect for making paracord weave bracelets and other projects is to combine colors. One of the best ways to blend colors is to splice two pieces of cord together. While this particular splice is pretty strong, you should still consider this two short pieces of cord rather than one long piece.

Take the two cords you want to splice side by side.

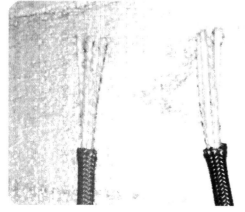

Pull out an inch of the inner cord and bring the bottoms of the cords up to the top, basically just go to the other side of the cords.

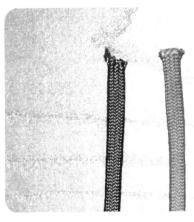

You may have to smooth the bottoms down until one inch of the core fibers retreats into the shell.

Take one of the cords and slide it into the other down to the filling. Heat the free fibers with a lighter until they close flush to the other cord.

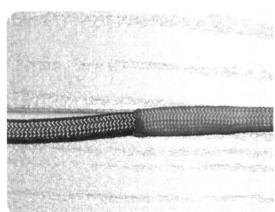

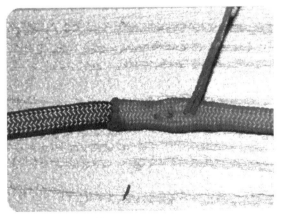

For added strength to the splice, stitch the middle of the splice with some strong thread.

30 Two Cord Splice

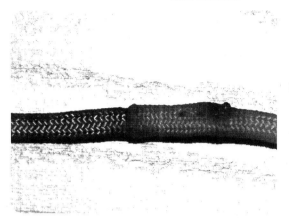

With a splice like this, this cord can be used for any one of the projects in the book, though I wouldn't suggest it for any sort of task requiring it to bear weight.

SLIDING TOGGLE

While the cobra knot shown earlier was tied around itself, it is possible to actually tie the knot around something else. When tied over another cord or cords, this free-floating cobra knot allows the inner strands to move about with some degree of freedom. This allows you to make survival bracelets and toggles that slide.

Start with your central cords, they can be anything.

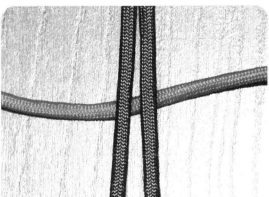

Place your length of paracord behind the central core.

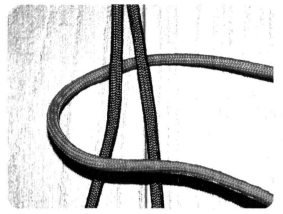

Bring one of the ends up and around the front.

Take the other and bring it behind, effectively tying an overhand knot over the core material.

Tighten the overhand knot and start tying knots like the normal cobra stitch.

To make a sliding toggle, tie knots until you have about four loop bumps on each side.

To finish the toggle, just seal ups the ends using the method of your choice. I suggest rubbing a little bit of candle wax to the central cord afterwards to allow the toggle to run smoothly.

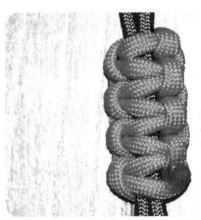

CHAPTER 2
THE SURVIVAL BRACELET

One of the things I love about paracord is that it is so useful. I have some in my car next to the duct tape, and I try to make sure that somehow I have at least a few feet at all times. The best way to keep some paracord on hand is by making a survival bracelet.

These bracelets are unique in that the central core can be quickly pulled out, making the knots easy to pull apart. Even a small bracelet can contain as much as seven feet of paracord, and a larger bracelet with two layers of cord can have as many as 20 feet, more than enough for a myriad of uses. Make a few of these, you never know when they might come in handy.

Loop and Knot

This is one of the simplest ways to make a survival bracelet. It has a few advantages. First, it is fairly compact, and though it only carries about seven to nine feet of cord, the reduced size is a bonus. The loop and knot closure requires no special hardware or findings, and there is no metal in this bracelet at all. Ideal for hiking, swimming, sailing, etc.. Double the knots like on page 95, and this bracelet can easily carry fifteen feet of cord.

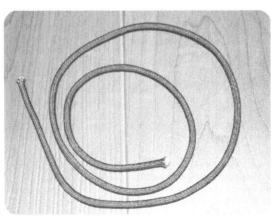

Start out with about two feet of cord. Choose whichever color you want for the inside. If your wrists are large, say over ten inches around, add another six inches.

THE SURVIVAL BRACELET

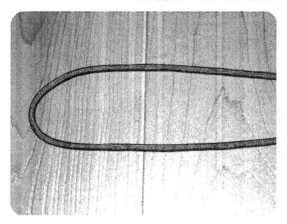

Find the center and then lay the ends down and measure out about half an inch more than your wrist measurement.

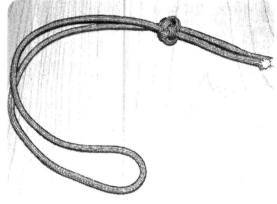

Tie a lanyard knot or overhand knot to the open ends and check the fit again.

You want it to be a little loose, with about enough room to fit a finger or two comfortably when it is around your wrist. When the knots are tied, the bracelet will become snug. If going double, make it a little larger.

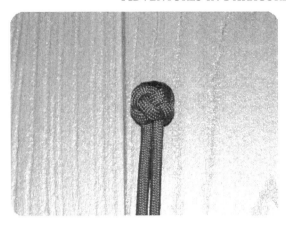

Trim and melt the end of the knot to clean it up.

Cut enough paracord to cover the length of the bracelet. Measure one foot for every inch you intend to cover plus a little extra. So if your wrist is eight inches, cut eight feet, six inches.

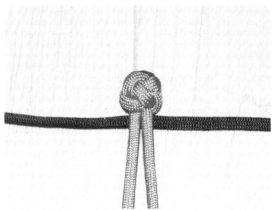

Find the center of your paracord and place it under the bracelet right below the knot.

38 LOOP AND KNOT

THE SURVIVAL BRACELET

Start by tying an overhand knot, making a sliding toggle.

Pull the lanyard knot out a little so that it has some room, then continue down to the end.

Continue knotting down to about an inch from the end, and then finish off the ends of the knots.

To put the bracelet on, place it on your wrist and then slip the loop over the knot.

When taking it off and on, try not to pull too hard on the knot end, as the core might slip out and the loop will get sucked into the cobra knots.

BUCKLE

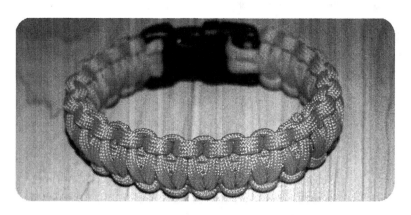

A side release buckle makes this bracelet easier to wear and attach to things, and allows every other part of the bracelet to be made of a single piece. The main downside is that keeping the bracelet from falling apart inadvertently requires some tweaking to keep the quick-disassembly feature of the survival bracelet intact. These bracelets, if made larger, also make good dog collars.

Any side release buckle will work for these bracelets. This particular one is a $^3/_4$ inch curved buckle. Check old backpacks and soft cases for buckles.

Measure out three feet plus a foot for every inch of bracelet. Find the center and pass it through the innermost (closest to the prongs) slot on the buckle from the bottom.

To make them easier to pass through the other side of the buckle, heat and pinch the ends of the paracord.

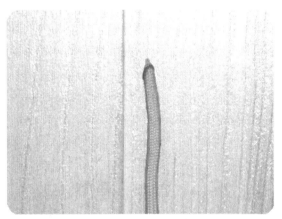

Pass the cords up through the buckle slot from the bottom.

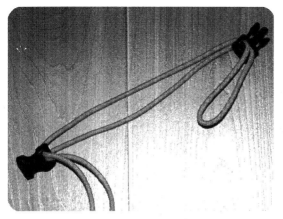

The bracelet should now look like this. Pull on the end loop to adjust the length between the two buckles. You want the cord plus the length of the buckle closed to measure $\frac{1}{2}$ an inch over your wrist size.

Once the bracelet is the right length, bring the loose ends from the bottom, making sure they are even with the rest of the bracelet.

Once everything is even, tie an over-hand knot and start tying cobra knots down the bracelet.

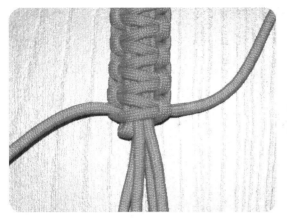

Once you reach the end of the loop that you knotted over, stop.

In order to fill the bracelet up and make it appear even, cut a length of paracord at least double the distance between the end of the loop and the bottom buckle.

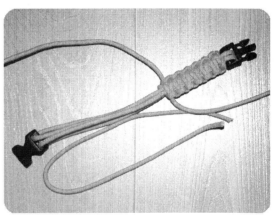

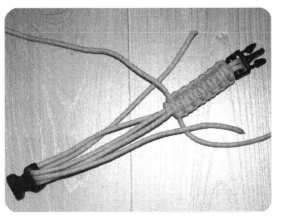

Pass it through the bottom buckle through the center, and line it up with the bracelet.

44 BUCKLE

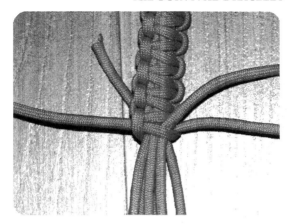

Continue tying knots, covering up the loop and the new cords.

Keep knotting until you reach the end, and tighten or loosen the middle cord now to make sure the three loops line up.

Finish up the end of the knots.

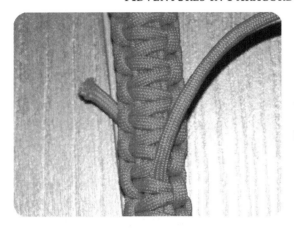

The middle cords will be sticking out of the top of the bracelet, so go back and trim them.

Here's the finished bracelet.

If you are planning on making a collar for a cat, shave down half of one of the prongs on the side. This will allow the buckle to come apart in case they get hung up on it.

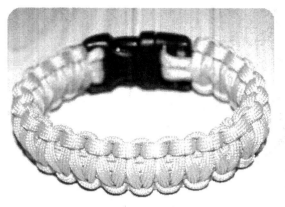

These also make good luggage tags. I've also used them for attaching things to my backpack when bike riding, hiking, etc..

Taking Them Apart

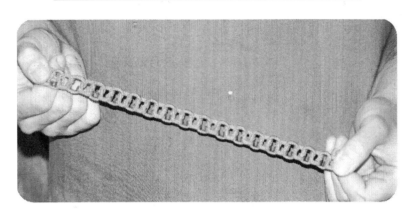

While any of the paracord bracelets, keychains, watch-bands, and lanyards can be pulled apart the same way they were put together, the survival bracelet has the added bonus of being easily taken apart.

By being able to remove the center filling, it opens the knots up, allowing them to come apart very easily. Here's how you do it.

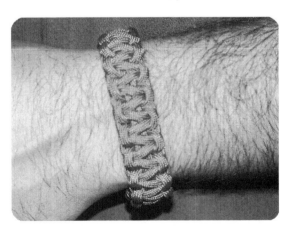

The loop and knot bracelet is the easiest to pull apart.

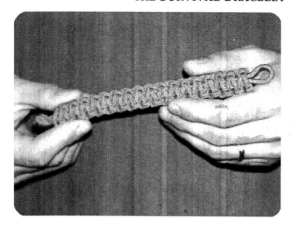

First, take it off of your wrist.

Next, grab hold of the knot with one hand, and grip the sides of the bracelet firmly with the other.

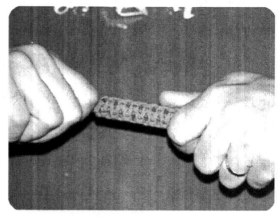

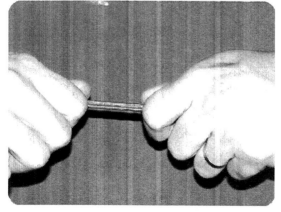

Pull hard and the core will come out.

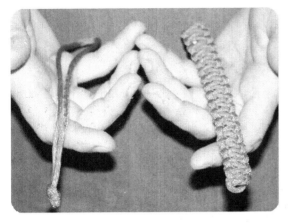

Without the center cord, the knots will become very loose.

Like this.

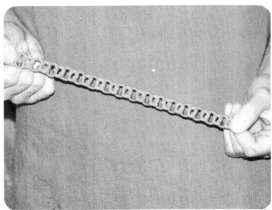

Simply untie the knots. For a faster method, a stick can be inserted and used to push the knots apart. This can be done in quick strokes and takes the knots out quickly.

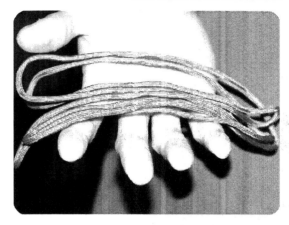

Once the knots are out, you have a handful of paracord, ready for anything.

The buckled bracelet is a little more complicated.

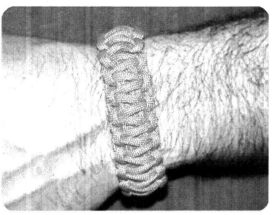

Locate the end with the small loop under the knots. In this bracelet, it is on the side with the prongs.

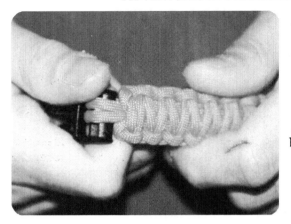

Grasp the pronged side in one hand, and the sides of the bracelet in the other.

With a rocking, side to side motion, pull until the loop comes out. Take the buckle off and flip the bracelet over.

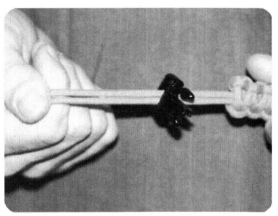

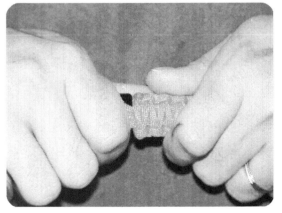

Grasp the other buckle and wiggle the cord back and forth to pull the loop through.

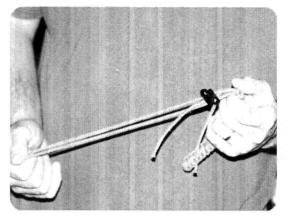

Once the loop starts coming out, grab it and pull it all the way out. Take the buckle off and pull the center cord running through the buckle out as well.

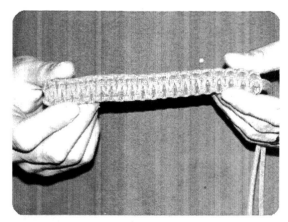

Turn the bracelet over and then pick the ends of the cords where they disappear into the bracelet out.

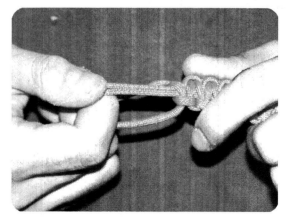

Like this.

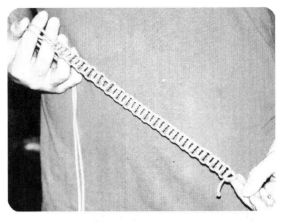

Once you've pulled the end out, the knots will open up. Now they can be easily pulled apart.

Now you have a good amount of paracord, a little extra scrap, and a buckle to use.

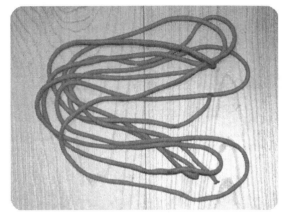

CHAPTER 3
THE PARACORD BRACELET

Aside from being extremely useful, paracord can also be fashionable. These bracelets are great for everyday wear. They are light, water-resistant, and come in whatever colors you can find.

The regular bracelet is great for men, and it contains anywhere from six to ten feet of paracord just in case. The slim bracelet has the internal strands pulled out, so it has a nice, sleek appearance and is great for kids and women. The loop and knot band is really simple, and is great for anyone.

PARACORD BRACELET

This bracelet is a great candidate for spliced cords, as the two-tone effect is very eye-catching. Like the buckled survival bracelet, these make great luggage tags and are good for attaching things to a pack or a belt. If made larger and the cords run through the loops one more time to double the thickness, these make excellent collars for large dogs.

You'll need a side release buckle and a length of paracord that is three feet plus a foot per inch of wrist size.

Find center, then push the loop from the top of the buckle down. Pass the ends through the loop, locking it in place.

On the other buckle, pass the ends through the buckle from top to bottom, and pull until the cord plus the buckles when closed equal half an inch over your wrist size.

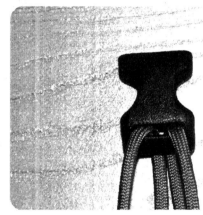

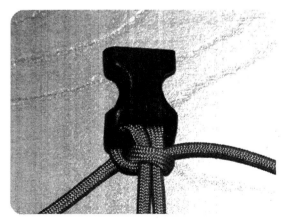

Start tying your knots, going all the way to the end.

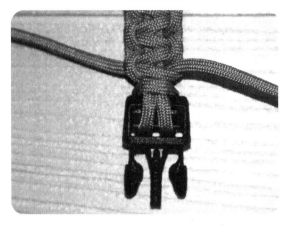

Once at the end, make sure the knots butt up against the bottom loop.

Finish up the ends and you are ready to go!

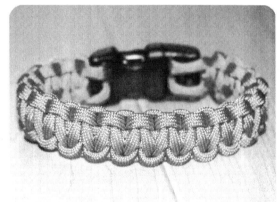

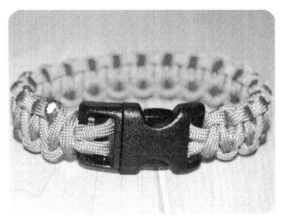

I have also made very, very long versions of these as legitimate straps for holding things down. In that case, steel claw clasps work well.

SLIM BRACELET

One of my wife's favorite bracelets, the slim bracelet is the same as the other except the inner strands are removed. This type of bracelet is very light and fits well against the wrist.

These bracelets look great as a solid color and with a two-cord splice. These also make good collars for very small dogs and cats. If making a collar for cat, buy a special side-release buckle specifically for them.

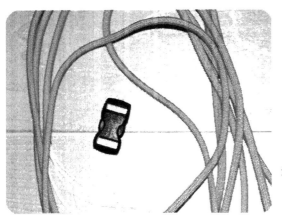

Start with your buckle and paracord. This buckle is a very small one, only half an inch wide. For the paracord, measure out two feet plus eight inches for every inch of length.

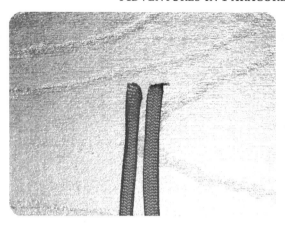

Pull out the inner strands of the paracord and melt the ends so that they will slide into the buckle easier.

Loop the center of the paracord through the top buckle.

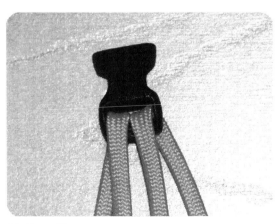

On the other end, run the ends of the cord through the other half of the buckle.

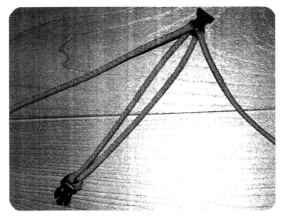

Adjust the bracelet now to your desired length. Go just about an eighth of an inch above your wrist measurement.

Begin knotting down to the end.

Because there is no core, the shell may twist like in the picture to the left. It's barely noticeable, but makes the weave look sloppy. Just keep this in mind, and try to keep the cords from twisting.

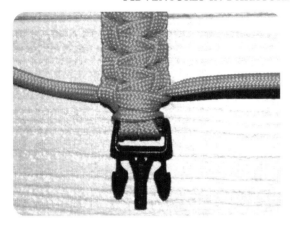

Once you reach the end,

Finish up the ends and you are done!

The bracelet without the cord's inside strands is probably one of the coolest looking of the paracord bracelets.

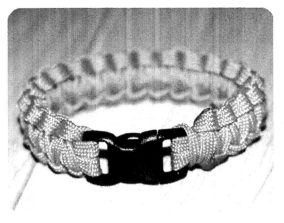

If you want to use a larger buckle, a second layer of knots will make the bracelet even with the $^3/_4$ buckle.

LOOP AND KNOT BAND

The loop and knot band is a very simple, small bracelet. It has only one single cord running in the core. For a core that is still small but offers the possibility of neater ends, follow the directions for the loop and knot survival bracelet, except pull out the core strands of the paracord.

Start by making a loop and then tying an overhand knot. The loop should be about half an inch long.

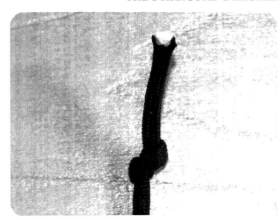

Measure from the other loop how long you want the core to be. It should be a little longer than your wrist size. Tie an overhand knot here.

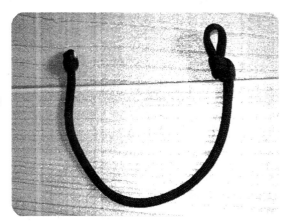

Clean up both knots by trimming and melting the excess.

Measure a length of paracord that is about a foot long per inch of bracelet length and remove the inner strands.

Center the cord under the end knot, then begin the cobra knot.

Before you go too far down, pull the knot up so that there is room for it to move.

Keep knotting until you reach the end, making sure the last knots are up against the overhand knot.

THE PARACORD BRACELET

Clean up the ends,
and you are done.

Chapter 4
THE WATCH BAND

When I was in college, my old time companion, a citizen titanium dive watch which I had worn for over five years, finally died. With it dead, I had to find a way to not miss all my classes, so I popped down to WallyWorld and picked up a cheap watch for five bucks.

Within a week, the band broke. Now I had two useless watches. At least the actual watch part of the cheap watch worked, but it had no band. Rather than take it back or get another one, I had an idea. Within a few minutes, I had a stylish paracord watch that was the envy of the floor.

Come to think of it, I think it got stolen that semester. Oh well, I have a better watch now. It cost $9.50.

FULL CORD

Making a full cord band requires using a watch that will allow six full strands of paracord to pass through. This usually only works with large, stainless steel dive watches or those large discount watches they sell at lower-end department stores.

If you can't find either, a watch with a raised back like this one works as well. The instructions are the same for all three.

You will need your watch and a side release buckle. This watch was very interesting. It is a watch slid over a slap bracelet. Remember those? I remember all the girls in elementary school had one.

It's kind of like those girly plastic lanyard things I used to play with. Wait. I know what you're thinking. This is paracord, it's manly! This is different!

That aside, you want to remove the existing watch band.

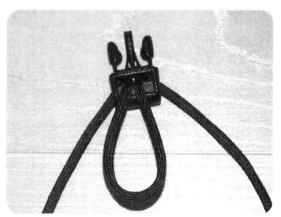

Take a length of paracord three feet long plus one foot for every inch of finished band. Find the center and pass it through the buckle slot.

THE WATCH BAND

Bring the ends of the cord through the loop and lock it into place.

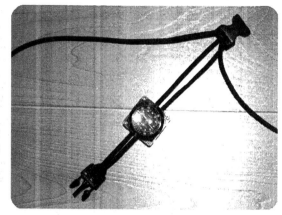

Run the ends of the cord through the watch and into the other buckle slot. Adjust it to the length of half an inch over your wrist size.

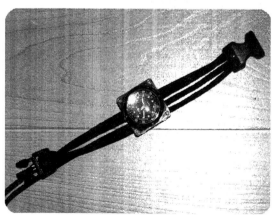

Pass the ends back through the watch again and to the other buckle.

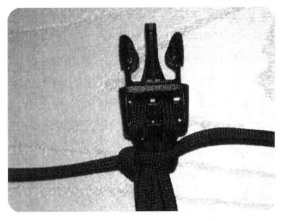

Begin tying your knots right below the buckle.

Keep going until you reach where you want the watch to sit.

Turn the watch over and bring the watch up to the end of the knots.

the Watch Band

Pass the ends of the cord through and pull it snug.

Continue the cobra knot below the watch.

Once you get down to the end, finish up the band.

Here is the finished watch band.

EMPTY CORD

This band, which is similar to the other, is suited for smaller watches that don't have the room for six full strands of cord to fit around the watch case.

If the band is left as a single line of cobra knots, it is perfect for larger women's watches and kid's watches. Doubling the knots and doing a king cobra stitch will give a larger, fuller band that is perfect for men's watches.

First, find yourself a watch. This watch is almost an exact copy of the one I had in college. The only difference is it cost more. Unlike the last one, the band is being removed forcibly.

Most watches of this style have little pins that can be pulled out by compressing the little springs on the ends.

Once you have your watch case, get a buckle and a length of cord. Start with four feet and then add two feet for every inch of band. If you are doing the single band, use a smaller buckle and half the paracord.

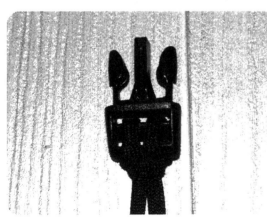

Remove the strands in your paracord, and loop the center around the top buckle like this.

Bring the ends of the cord up and around, through the buckle slot and back through the loop to double the cord in the buckle and keep it from sliding from side to side.

Run the cord through the pins and behind the watch case.

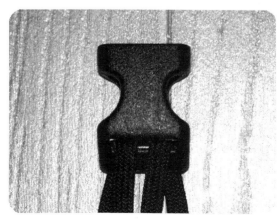

On the other end, pass the ends of the cords through the bottom buckle. Now is the time to adjust for the length of your bracelet. About a half and inch larger than your wrist is good.

Bring the ends back up and loop it again to fill up the slot.

Tie an overhand knot and begin the cobra stitch.

Stop once you're down to where you want the watch to sit.

Pass the ends of the cord under the pins and behind the back of the case.

Flipped over, this is what it should look like. Pull the cord tight so that the cords stay neat and even.

Continue tying knots to the end.

If you want the band to be skinny, you can finish it up here.

If you want a fuller band, start tying another set of cobra knots, making a king cobra knot. If you already finished the thinner band, you can use another piece of paracord as if it were a sliding toggle.

Once you've gotten back down to the watch case, flip the watch over.

Pass the ends of the cord under the pins to rest next to the other cords. Pull them tight to keep them even.

Continue tying knots until you reach the bottom.

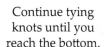

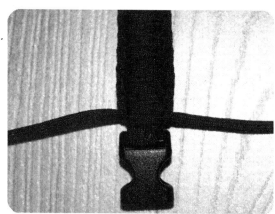

Finish the ends, and you are done.

LOOP AND KNOT

This final band is almost exactly the same as the loop and knot survival bracelet. As such, it can be pulled apart just like the survival bracelet. This small band is great for smaller men's watches and smaller ladies watches. For really small watches, removing the inner fibers in the central cords will usually allow them to fit.

Start with about two feet of cord and your watch.

Measure half an inch over your wrist measurement and tie a lanyard knot.

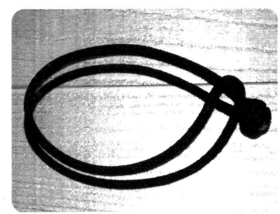

Clean up the end of the knot.

Slide the watch case onto the cord.

Cut a length of cord that is one foot long for every inch of bracelet length and place the center under the knot.

Start the cobra stitch just below the knot.

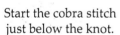

Continue down to where you want the watch to sit, then flip the watch over.

Instead of going under the pins, we'll be running the ends of the cords under the core strands.

Criss-cross the cords underneath the central strands like this.

Pull it down tight, but not so tight that the pins get ripped out or bent.

THE WATCH BAND

Flip the watch over and continue the knots.

Finish the end, clean everything up, and you are done.

CHAPTER 5
<u>KEYCHAINS</u>

As a kid, I never understood the concept of keys. When I finally had to carry a key to get into the house, suddenly my appreciation for keys was greatly magnified. Especially when I had to sit outside for an hour or so for my mom or dad to come home and let me in cause I forgot my keys.

Not much has changed since then, and my forgetfulness with keys is still an issue. Though since I put a bright neon blue paracord keychain on my keys three years ago, I haven't lost them once! And only forgot them five times! Which for me is a big accomplishment.

This chapter goes over a basic little key fob, a cool spiral keychain, and a keychain that allows for detachment for a valet key or for attaching to a belt or pocket.

SIMPLE KEYCHAIN

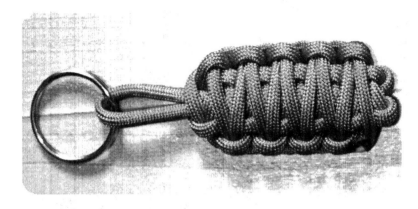

This little keychain is very versatile. You could loop beads, a watch, really anything on the end. It also makes a good ID tag for luggage, and if made without the inner strands (or with), it makes a great zipper pull.

Aside from all that, it makes a pretty spiffy key holder. Make it in really bright colors and it will get a little harder to misplace your keys (hopefully).

Start with three feet of paracord and a keychain ring. You could always make the keychain first, the slide the ring on later.

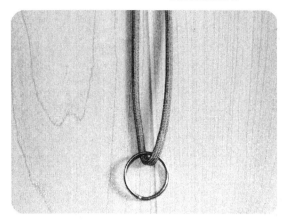

Find center, and place the ring at center.

Start your cobra knot at 3 inches from the ring. Adjust this if you want the keychain longer or shorter.

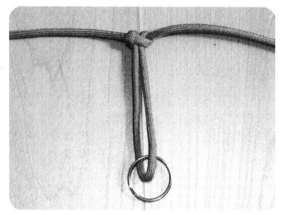

Keep knotting for two inches. You could go further or go less, just use more or less cord respectively.

Once the knotting is finished, finish up the ends and you are done.

Or you can do a king cobra stitch. Either start with double the cord, like on the left, or add cord on top.

Turn the keychain over, and pull the ends tight.

Make a cobra knot, and tighten it so that it falls into the creases, but not so much it separates the inner cords.

Continue down until you reach the end.

Clean up the ends and you are done. The keychain on the right used a separate cord over the base cord.

DNA KEYCHAIN

While I call this the DNA keychain, this is really a spiral stitch. A spiral stitch is what happens if you don't alternate the knot direction, resulting in a stack of granny knots instead of a stack of square knots.

This resulting spiral looks a lot like the DNA models you see everywhere. This keychain is great due to its rounded body and offers a good grip on your keys. It's perfect for the mad scientist in your life!

Start with 4 feet of paracord. Find the center and place the ring at center.

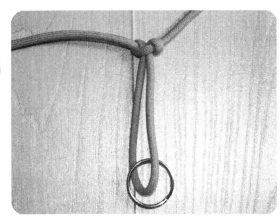

Start with a knot at 3 inches from the ring.

Let's get up-close and take a look at how the spiral stitch works. This is how the cords should look before the first knot is tightened.

After tightening. Notice how the left cord went over the front.

DNA KEYCHAIN 95

Now here is the second knot. Notice how instead of the right cord going over the front like in the cobra stitch, the left cord is, again, in front.

Pull it tight and you will see that the second knot lines up a little off from the center, making the spiral.

Continue going down.

96 DNA KEYCHAIN

If you want to mix things up, you could reverse the spin at any time by alternating the knot, like this.

With that reversal, you end up with this double twist keychain. Simply stay in one direction for a single twist.

Double Keychain

The double keychain is basically two keychains attached by a side release buckle. This way you can have one side attached to a belt or bag, and the other to your keys. Or have one side hold a valet key so you don't have to hand over all your keys. The possibilities are endless. These make great straps for things that you need to use freely. If made longer, they can be used to make a bracelet with the two loops holding a charm or ID tag.

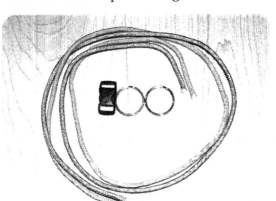

Start with two lengths of paracord roughly one foot per inch of length each, a buckle, and two key rings.

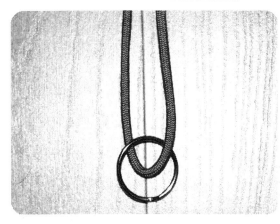

Starting with your first one, center the ring on the paracord.

Pass the ends of the paracord through the buckle slot.

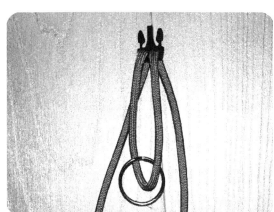

Adjust the amount of cord in the loop to get your desired length, giving a little room for the end loop.

Begin the cobra knot.

Stop about half an inch from the end, to give the ring some space to move.

Clean up the ends and the first half is finished.

100 DOUBLE KEYCHAIN

Repeat for the second half. I like to make one longer and one shorter, though you can adjust them to whatever size suits your needs.

This keychain is great for a valet key. Put all your keys on one side, and the valet key on the other. When you check into the hotel, unbuckle the keychain, and hand over only your valet key.

CHAPTER 6
LANYARDS AND STRAPS

Among its uses, paracord also makes great lanyards and straps. If you need to keep something close at hand or secured from slipping from your grasp, paracord is great.

In this chapter we'll be making a neck lanyard for holding keys, ID badges, or whatever else you want on your neck, a simple strap for keeping things to your wrist, and a handy neck cord that keeps your glasses from hitting the ground if they fall off your face.

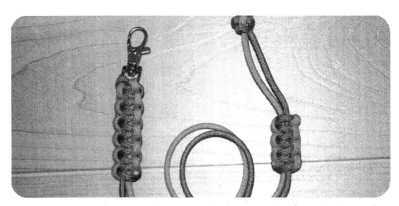

Back in college, I needed to have my keys on me at all times. No matter what I was doing, I needed to have my keys, because if I found myself in the forest at midnight, there would be nobody to open my dorm building's door. Even a trip to the bathroom could result in disaster if my room mate decided to step out. To solve this, I kept my keys around my neck with this handy lanyard. I only forgot them once. Standing outside for an hour, naked... Brrrr.

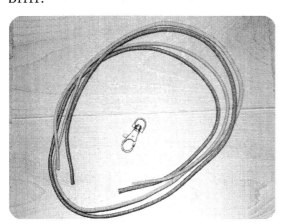

Start with two pieces of paracord four feet long and a claw clasp. This is a great time to use two colors as you don't need to do a splice.

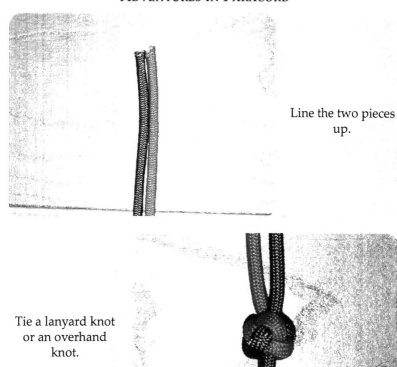

Line the two pieces up.

Tie a lanyard knot or an overhand knot.

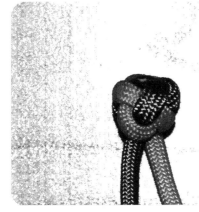

Finish the knot by trimming and melting the ends.

On the other end, run the cords through until there is eighteen inches between the clasp and the lanyard knot.

Begin tying your cobra knot.

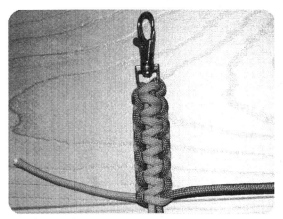

Continue for about two to three inches or however long you want the cobra stitch to be.

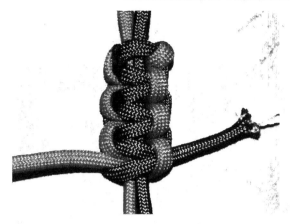

On the main cords, make a sliding toggle.

Finish the ends and now you have a stylish adjustable neck lanyard.

WRIST STRAP

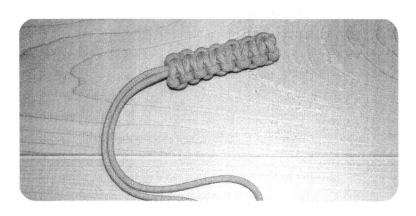

This strap is useful for adding a little extra grip to small knives, keeping expensive cameras from falling out of your hand, or even identifying your suitcase on the conveyor.

It is simple in that all you need is a length of paracord. Metals rings are not required, though a small ring on the cobra stitch side makes attaching to cell phones and other electronics easier.

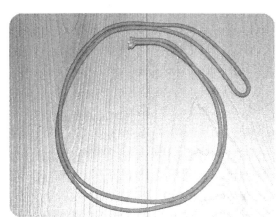

Start with five feet of cord, and find the center.

Place an overhand knot 3 inches away from the end of the loop, plus however long you want the strap opening to be.

Finish up the ends.

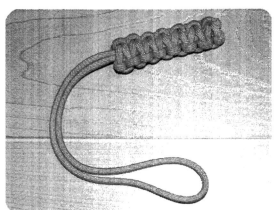

Here's the finished strap. Easy, huh?

108 WRIST STRAP

This little knife is made much more practical with the addition of this strap. These straps can also make interesting Christmas ornaments!

GLASSES STRAP

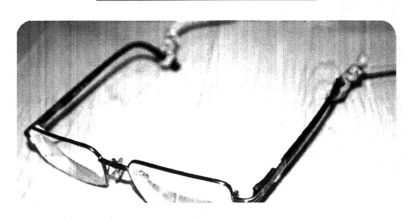

I wear glasses all the time. As a result of shaping and building tiny bone hooks and reading into the wee hours of the morning regularly, my eyesight is fast approaching blindness. In fact, without them all I see are blurred colors during the day and star bursts at night.

That is why it is important to me to keep my glasses on my face and not broken on the floor. This strap does just that.

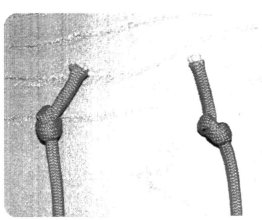

Start with a thirty inch length of para-cord. Tie an over-hand knot in each end.

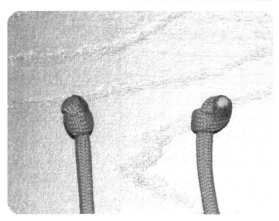

Trim and melt the ends down.

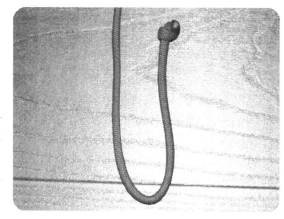

Take one end and form a slight loop like this.

Tie an overhand knot just under the end knot.

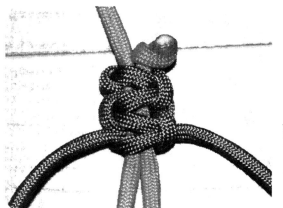

Tie cobra knots until you reach two bumps on each side.

Tie one last cobra knot, except tie it around the side of the loop with the knot.

This will keep the loop from accidentally being pulled through the toggle.

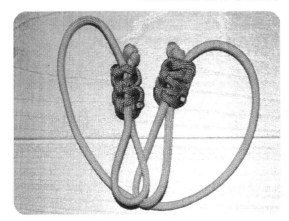

Trim and clean up the ends and you are done.

To use, simply place the ends of your frames into each loop and pull it tight.

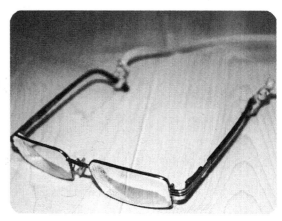

CHAPTER 7
CORD WRAPPING

One of the most basic uses for paracord is to wrap things with it. You can use it to enhance the grip on knives, tools, brooms, spears, etc.. Wrapping is also good for adding cushion to poles, as well as for turning anything into an oversized survival bracelet for carrying cord around.

The four wraps in this chapter consist of a basic wrap which is good for adding grip and cushion to handles and cylindrical objects, a looped and crossed over wrap ideal for knife handles, and a cobra wrap which can turn anything into a survival item. Think a survival belt. A hundred feet of cord as opposed to only ten. Sounds good, huh?

BASIC

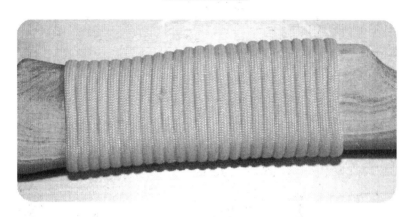

The basic cord wrap is one that I find extremely useful. This wrap is a great thing for increasing the comfort and grip for tools like hammers, axes, saws, etc. It can also help protect the wrapped surface from damage due to bumps or falls.

This wrap is also good for lashing things together, which is a great use for the inner paracord strands in a survival situation.

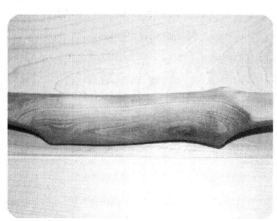

Start with whatever you need wrapped. In this case, it's a selfbow handle.

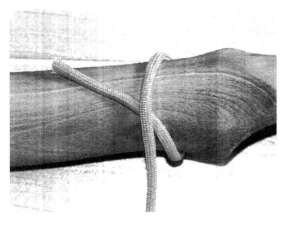

Place one end of the cord down the handle about halfway, then loop the longer end around it.

Loop it a few more times and then pull the short end tight, tightening the end of the wrap.

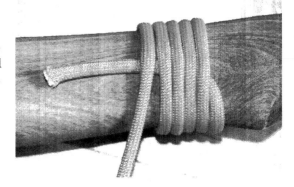

Keep going down until you cover the short end.

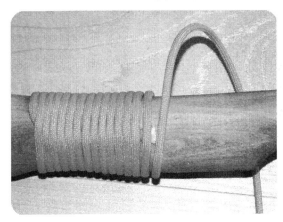

Now make a loop as if you were going to wrap around once more.

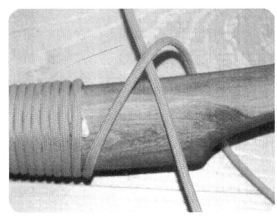

Bring the end up and through the loop you made and pull it so that you have a wrapped loop under the top loop.

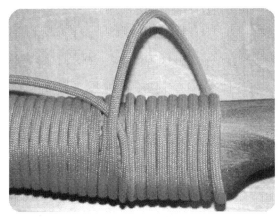

Keep wrapping until the handle is covered.

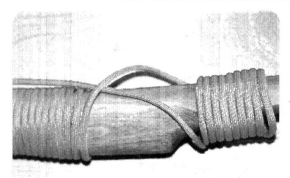

Slide the loops over to the side and bring the end of the cord so that it is under the wrap.

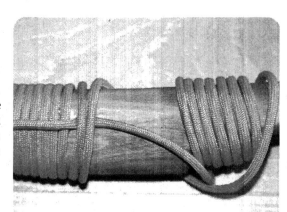

Now start winding the loop around and it will move the loops from the back of the handle to the center, covering the end of the cord.

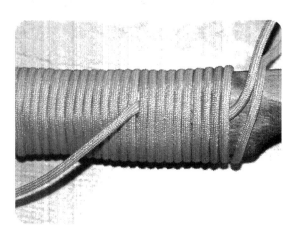

Keep wrapping tightly until you reach the end.

Pull the cord tight, which will tighten up the ends.

Trim the end sticking out, and you are done with the basic wrap.

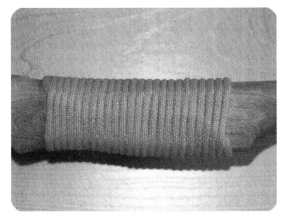

LOOPED

The first time I saw this particular handle wrap, it was in college. The knife in question was cheap, made in China, and had a poorly wrapped handle. After it came loose and unraveled, the friend who owned it asked me if I could fix it, since I like making things.

After re-wrapping it in a similar style to the one here, I realized how much extra grip this wrap affords. I was hooked.

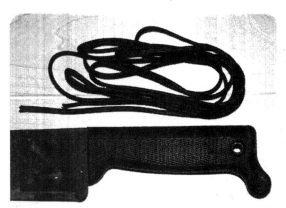

Start by wrapping cord around the item to be wrapped with a basic wrap, just to determine how long it needs to be.

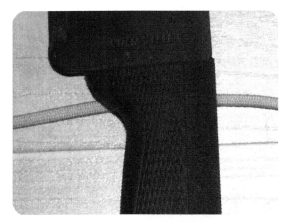

Lay the cord behind
your handle.

Cross one cord over
the other.

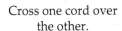

Cross the cords back
so that the left side
goes back to the left
and the right goes
back to the right.

Pull that tight and then flip the handle over.

An easier way to do this is to lay both cords down,

then twist them around and pulling the ends tight,

Cord Wrapping

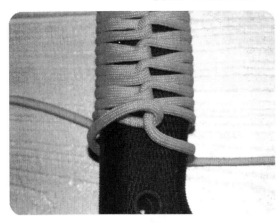

Continue wrapping down to the end.

Finish the end, in this case the tucking under works the best. Use a loop to assist in tucking the end under.

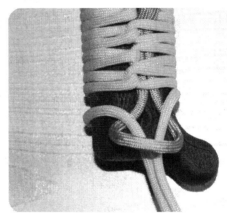

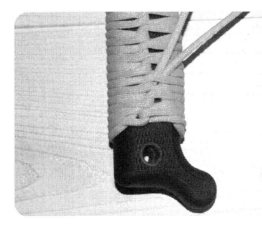

Like this.

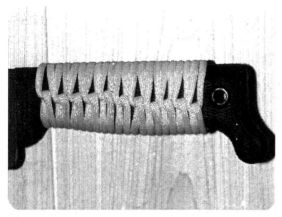

Here's the finished wrap. It offers a lot of grip, as each finger has a place to dig into. The downside is that this grip can dig into the palm after a while. I do not suggest it for axe, hatchet, or hammer handles.

CROSSED OVER

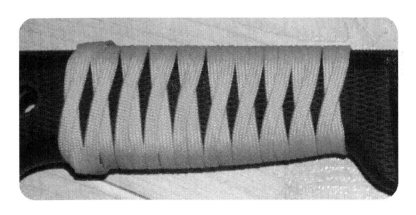

The crossed over wrap is a nice wrap where the purpose is more looks and less grip. While still enhancing the grip of whatever you are wrapping, the empty cord lays flat, which does not dig into the palm as much.

This wrap is similar to a style used on Japanese swords, which is a simpler version of the twisted version most people are familiar with.

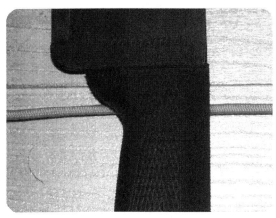

Start by wrapping cord around the item to be wrapped with a basic wrap, just to determine how long it needs to be. Remove the core from your cord and place the center behind the handle.

Start alternating the cords, bringing one over the other to cross them over each other.

Turn the handle around and continue on the other side.

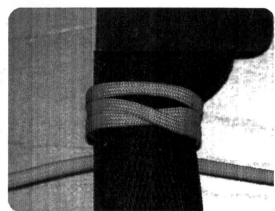

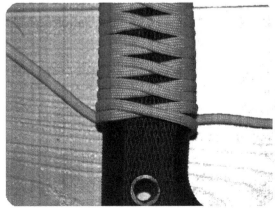

Keep going until you reach the end.

126 CROSSED OVER

Cord Wrapping

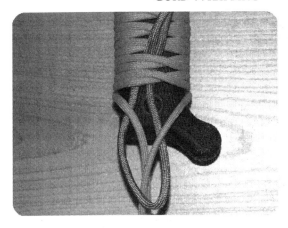

This is how you'd finish the wrap by tucking the ends under.

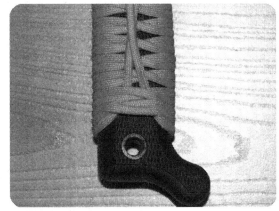

Once the end is finished clean it up.

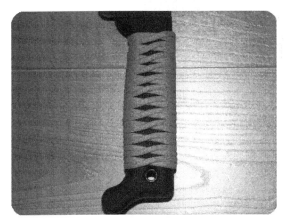

Enjoy your finished wrap. This wrap looks very impressive on broom handles for some reason. I don't know why.

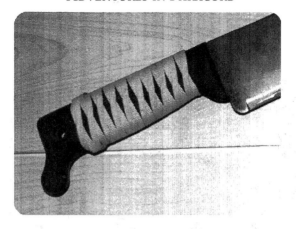

COBRA

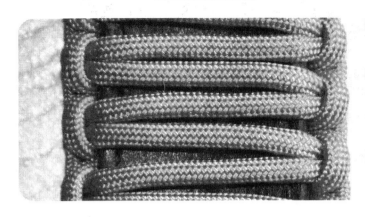

The cobra knot itself can be used to make a decorative and practical wrap. This wrap is ideal for belts, thin-handled knives, utensils, and basically anything flat.

By putting this wrap over a belt, you can turn a regular leather or nylon webbing belt into a super survival belt, which can hold as much as one-hundred feet of paracord. Now that is useful. You can also still use the belt afterwards.

Start out with whatever you want to wrap. In this case, it is a belt.

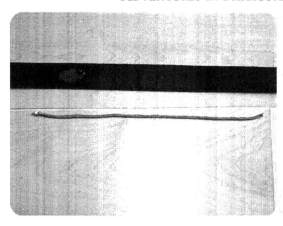

Cut a piece of paracord one foot long.

Tie knots until you can't tie anymore. Measure how much distance you covered. Now you know how much distance you can cover with one foot.

Use that previous measurement to ensure you have enough cord to finish the wrap.

Cord Wrapping

Start knotting, going all the way to the end.

Once you are at the end, finish the ends up and you are done!

THANK YOU

I would like to take some time to thank everyone who made this book possible, whether through direct encouragement or in spirit.

You, the reader. Without you, all this would be pointless.

To my wife, Angela, who was my consultant, model, camerawoman, slave-driver, cheering section, agent, and overall companion on this journey. Without you, none of this would be possible. I'd probably be in the forest right now, slinging stones at unsuspecting trees.

To my son, Levi, who was also in the cheering section. Who would have thought I could write a book while also changing diapers and imitating a circus clown. I may not be a clown, but I think I'll keep the shoes. Lots of extra toe room.

To my old college room mate, Cheyne (sounds like Shane) who always supported my crazy creative side, despite waking up every morning and having to shake the wood dust from your sheets and hair. If not for you, I don't think I would have tried the cobra knot.

To my high-school friend and college savior Chris, whose love for the outdoors meant that I eventually spent most of my time in the forest and not in class. Thanks for letting me fix your knife, as well as taking me to the army surplus store. Also, the food was great too.

To my parents, who supported me even when I spent most of my time not in class. You guys rock.

To everyone else I call friend, my warmest thanks.

About the Author

Nicholas Tomihama was born in Honolulu, where he lived until graduating high school. From there he went to Hilo on the island of Hawaii (the Big Island) to study business management at the University of Hawaii at Hilo.

Even before going to college, he had a knack for making things and working with his hands, perhaps coming from his father who was a jeweler and general jack-of-all-trades. In high school, Nicholas made hand-turned wooden pens, collected coins, fossils, and toyed around with his father's hunting bow.

In Hilo, Nicholas was exposed to the party life and turned away from it, instead passing his time exploring the island and getting to his Hawaiian heritage. He began researching and studying native Hawaiian crafts, carving bone hooks, crafting woven slings, and other Hawaiian arts.

After becoming more interested with craft than education, Nicholas returned to Oahu without a degree and married his high school sweetheart, who had kept up with him in a long-distance relationship for the duration of his stay in Hilo.

Nicholas now lives on Oahu with his wife and young son, Levi. He is an artist who makes hand-crafted bows and arrows and enjoys the sport of archery. He is also an avid reader and prolific writer, who recently published his first book, <u>The Backyard Bowyer</u>, which teaches how to build simple wooden bows for the complete novice.

CHAPTER VIII
BONUS TRACK

Welcome to the bonus track! Don't mind me, I'm just doing a little archery practice. And speaking of archery, this chapter has a couple of bow-related uses for paracord.

First up is how to use paracord as a bow string. This works great for kid bows, but can also be used for heavier bows and for making a bow in the wilderness. Not the best string, but at lower weights it does a decent enough job.

Then we have a string keeper for helping keep your bow string from falling off the bow when it is unstrung. It can also double as a limb silencer to cut down on limb noise and vibration slightly.

Emergency Bow String

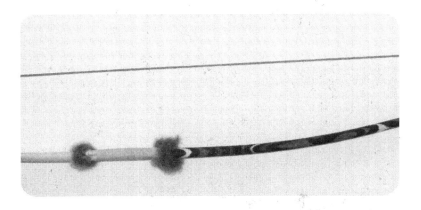

While you should always take care of your bow string, accidents do happen, and they do sometimes break or at least need replacing before they do. And while you should have a backup string, sometimes it's not with you or it needs replacing too.

When it comes down to that, a length of paracord can serve as a legitimate string. Due to the elasticity of the nylon, though, don't expect too much. This string not only will stretch when firing, but will creep a lot and the knots will need to be adjusted periodically.

If making a string, use 550 cord as it stretches less and has a higher weight bearing than 650 cord. While this works alright for longbows up to about 50 pounds, the stretch is hard to overcome on recurves without ruining your bow by flexing the limbs back too far.

Start by tying a sliding knot. To do the knot, start with the end of your paracord.

Bring the end around and under itself creating a loop.

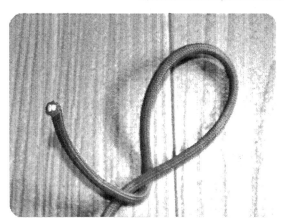

Bring the end up and over itself.

Then tuck the end back under and into the loop.

Bring the end down over the loop and then back under the main loop and into the small loop it makes.

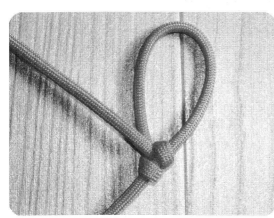

Tighten this knot, creating your loop. This will be the bottom loop of your string.

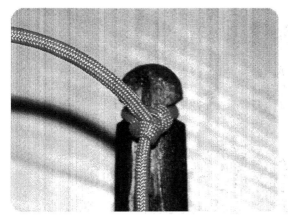

Slip it over the bottom nock of your bow and pull it tight.

Lay the string down the length of the bow, holding approximately a palm's width away from the nock. Pull the string until it no longer stretches as easily, but keep your thumb on the same spot.

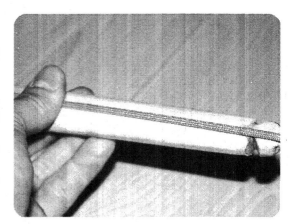

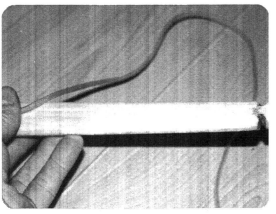

Let go of the tension on the string, letting your thumb follow the string as it relaxes.

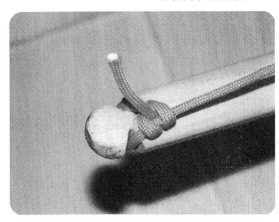

Go down about five inches from that point and tie a second knot.

When strung, the string will stretch out. On heavier bows, that initial distance from string loop to nock should be longer to allow for string stretch.

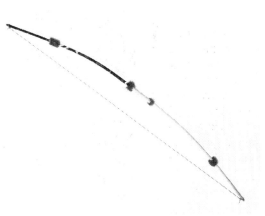

STRING KEEPER

If you shoot a stickbow like me, you will notice that when the bow is unstrung, the string tends to move around and sometimes slips off the bottom nock.

To prevent the string from moving around when the bow is unstrung, a simple row of cobra knots will help keep the string in place.

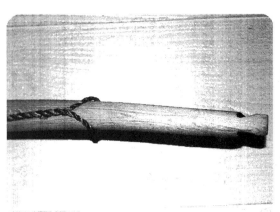

Start by slipping the string loop off of your bow's nock.

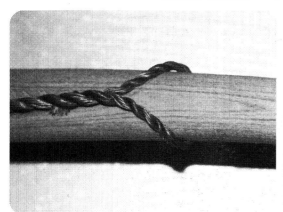

Hold it so that the string won't come off the bottom nock, but it's not tight enough to put tension on the bow or string.

Tie an overhand knot just below the string loop.

Take the string off and tighten the knot.

Tie cobra knots down to about three or four inches. You can do less or more. I find that a few of these down the limbs helps with limb noise and vibration if you have any.

Clean up the ends and your string keeper is done! Over are the days of bows strings tangling up on the bow rack!

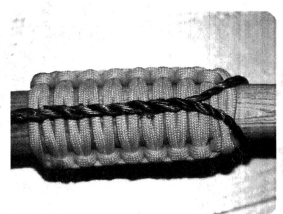

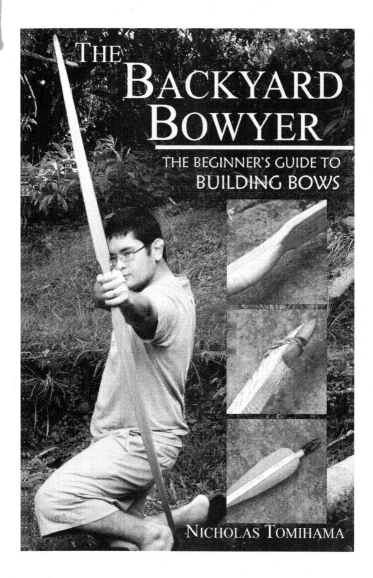

THE BACKYARD BOWYER

THE BEGINNER'S GUIDE TO BUILDING BOWS

NICHOLAS TOMIHAMA

IF YOU'VE EVER WANTED TO BUILD YOUR OWN WOODEN BOW, THE BACKYARD BOWYER IS READY TO TEACH YOU HOW! WITH OVER THREE HUNDRED PICTURES AND STEP-BY-STEP INSTRUCTIONS, THE BACKYARD BOWYER MAKES CRAFTING YOUR VERY FIRST WOODEN BOW A SIMPLE AND ENRICHING EXPERIENCE WITHOUT BREAKING THE BANK.

Made in the USA
Lexington, KY
04 August 2012